UNDERSTANDING

PAST LIFE

REGRESSION

THERAPY

Unlocking The Mysteries Of The Soul To Uncover The Power Within, Navigate Techniques, Embrace Healing And Self-Discovery, Transformative Insights And More

DR. KARSON BRYAN

DISCLAIMER

This book's content is meant to be used solely for general informative purposes. Despite having taken every precaution to guarantee the content's accuracy, the author disclaims all duty and responsibility for any errors or omissions. It is recommended that readers exercise caution and, if needed, seek expert guidance. Any and all liability for losses, damages, or other outcomes arising from the use of the material included in this book is disclaimed by the author and publisher. All referenced product names and trademarks are the property of their respective owners and are merely cited for identification. Any likeness to real people or things is entirely accidental. Since it is a work of fiction, this book should not be used as a substitute for professional, legal, or medical advice. It is advised that readers seek advice on particular issues from qualified experts."

Please make sure that this disclaimer is modified to fit the particular requirements and subject matter of your book. Seeking advice from a legal expert is also a smart option if you have any questions or require a more thorough disclaimer for your specific book.

TABLE OF CONTENTS

CHAPTER ONE

PAST LIFE REGRESSION THERAPY

INTRODUCTION

THE CAPTIVATING FIELD OF REGRESSION THERAPY TO PAST LIVES

The fascinating and contentious topic of past life regression therapy explores the complexities of human consciousness and the possibility that our souls have lived other incarnations. It is a therapy method that uses guided meditation or hypnosis to discover and investigate a person's purported past lives. Even while the scientific world continues to argue and be skeptical about it, it has attracted a sizable following and piqued the curiosity of individuals who believe in reincarnation and the potential therapeutic benefits of revisiting former life experiences.

MEANING OF PAST LIFE REGRESSION

The idea of reincarnation the conviction that the soul can reincarnate over time into many bodies and experiences—lays the foundation of past-life regression therapy. As a therapeutic approach, past life regression aims to assist people in gaining access to the memories and experiences of these purported past incarnations. Practitioners in this field claim that by exploring these memories from past lives, individuals can gain insight, heal emotional and physical issues, and achieve a deeper understanding of their current life's purpose and challenges. This is typically achieved through a relaxed and suggestible state, often induced through deep hypnosis or guided meditation, which means the person can access memories or experiences from their "past lives."

THE BACKGROUND OF REGRESSION TO PAST LIVES

The origins of past life regression can be found in spiritual traditions and ancient cultures. For thousands of years, reincarnation has been a fundamental component of many religious systems, including Buddhism and Hinduism. It has long been believed in many traditions that the soul travels through a cycle of birth and rebirth, accruing karma and experiences during each lifetime. The notion of reincarnation and past incarnations became more popular in the West during the 1800s, thanks to the introduction of these ideas by Helena Petrovna Blavatsky's Theosophical Society.

However, the development of past life regression therapy as a therapeutic modality started in the 1950s and 1960s. The field's pioneers, including renowned American psychic Edgar Cayce and, more recently, psychiatrist Dr. Brian Weiss, promoted the use of hypnosis and regression treatment to retrieve memories of past lives. The 1988 publication of Dr. Weiss's book "Many Lives, Many Masters" popularized this technique and generated debate as well as curiosity.

THE SCIENCE OF REGRESSION TO PAST LIVES

The scientific underpinnings of past life regression therapy are still divisive and controversial. Some who disagree contend that the memories that are recovered in regression sessions may just be fabrications made to satisfy the client's expectations or the result of the person's imagination, influenced by suggestions made by the therapist. The claims of past life recollection, according to skeptics, are not supported by any empirical data.

On the other hand, proponents of past life regression contend that anecdotal data from patients reporting notable therapeutic advantages is not to be discounted. They cite instances in which patients assert that receiving regression treatment led to the resolution of long-standing mental and physical problems or provided new perspectives on their present-day struggles.

Past life regression therapy is an intriguing and mysterious topic that addresses profoundly held notions about reincarnation, the nature of consciousness, and the human experience. Despite having roots in antiquated spiritual traditions, its application in modern therapy has produced ardent believers as well as detractors. The science underlying former life regression is still up for debate and investigation in the rapidly changing fields of human psychology and spirituality, as is the question of whether past life memories are genuine or the result of the mind.

CHAPTER TWO

COMPREHENDING FORMER LIVES

THE IDEA OF REINCARNATION

For ages, people of many cultures and religions have held varying versions of the concept of reincarnation. The fundamental tenet of reincarnation is that a person's soul or consciousness reincarnates into a different body following death. The soul may transcend the cycle and unite with a higher spiritual reality once it achieves a stage of spiritual enlightenment or perfection. This cycle of birth, death, and reincarnation continues until that point.

The idea that a person's past deeds, or karma, affect their current life's circumstances is frequently associated with the concept of reincarnation. Stated differently, an individual's experiences and obstacles in every lifetime stem from their previous actions and decisions.

A lot of beliefs about reincarnation are based on this idea of cause and consequence.

CULTURAL AND RELIGIOUS VIEWPOINTS

Reincarnation is accepted by a wide range of societies worldwide and is not exclusive to any one culture or religion. For example, reincarnation is a deeply held belief in Hinduism and is intimately related to the concept of karma. Hindus hold that the soul goes through a succession of births and deaths to achieve moksha or freedom from the material world, and ultimately end the cycle.

Though its understanding of reincarnation is different from Hinduism's, Buddhism too believes in it. Buddhists hold that there is an endless cycle of birth and rebirth that is brought about by the accumulation of karma. The cycle terminates when a person reaches Nirvana or enlightenment.

With roots in Abrahamic religions like Christianity, Judaism, and Islam, many Western societies, in contrast, have a more linear conception of life and death. Generally speaking, these faiths impart the belief in a single lifetime, followed by an afterlife that could include either heaven or hell. Within these religions, however, there have been individuals and mystical movements who have investigated the idea of reincarnation.

EVIDENCE FOR REINCARNATION

There is disagreement about the evidence for reincarnation, with proponents and opponents putting forth different arguments. Anecdotal evidence of people claiming to remember previous lives is frequently cited by proponents of reincarnation, particularly when those reports involve small children. These narratives occasionally contain precise information about names, places, events, and experiences from their previous lives that are challenging to interpret conventionally.

Studies on reincarnation have also been carried out by scientists such as Dr. Ian Stevenson, who gathered a large number of cases of youngsters recalling vivid recollections of previous lifetimes. These studies are frequently challenged, though, due to methodological issues and the possibility of suggestion or false recollections.

On the other hand, detractors contend that it is difficult to embrace the idea of reincarnation due to the absence of solid scientific proof. They argue that other psychological and cultural elements, such as suggestion, imagination, or assimilation of stories from others, can often account for the purported recollections of past lives.

Several civilizations and religions throughout history have accepted the complicated and nuanced idea of reincarnation.

CHAPTER THREE

MEMORIES FROM PREVIOUS LIVES AND THE SUBCONSCIOUS MIND

COMPREHENDING FORMER LIVES

For millennia, people have been captivated by the idea of reincarnation or memories of previous life. Numerous religions, such as Buddhism, Hinduism, and various New Age ideologies, support the notion that people have lived many lives. The study of past lives often touches on several important ideas, even though these beliefs may differ among cultures and spiritual traditions. These include how memories are stored, how to access memories from past lives, recurring themes and experiences in past life regression, going back in time to revisit historical periods, relationships and connections between lifetimes, unresolved issues, and karmic lessons.

How Memories Are Stored: The preservation of memories from previous lives is a fascinating topic. Reincarnation proponents contend that rather than being preserved in the physical brain, these memories are instead kept in a person's soul or awareness. These memories are thought to be ingrained in the soul and transfer over from one existence to the next. The concept is that these memories are an integral part of a person's spiritual essence, however, the method by which they are accessed can differ.

Regression to a past life, meditation, and hypnosis are common methods used to access memories from previous lives. By putting a person in a calm or altered state of awareness, past life regression enables them to investigate former lives. Through the procedure, memories that have been buried can come to the surface, revealing relationships, traumas, and past experiences.

There is disagreement over the scientific validity of these methods, but many people report having had life-changing experiences that have led to deep insights and emotional healing.

COMMON THEMES AND EXPERIENCES IN PAST LIFE REGRESSION

Numerous themes and experiences that cut beyond cultural and geographic borders have been identified in past life regression sessions. People frequently talk about seeing important people from their former incarnations, feeling strong emotions related to unsolved problems, or even feeling as though they recognize a location or era from a past life. These common experiences raise the possibility that there are aspects of the human experience that are universal, transcending individual lives and adding to humanity's collective understanding.

Revisiting Historical Periods The capacity to go back in time to historical periods is one of the more fascinating features of recollections of past lives.

Individuals who partake in previous life regression frequently recount vivid memories of living in various historical periods, which can offer insightful historical perspectives. These memories may include attire descriptions, social mores, or even involvement in historical events. It's debatable whether these memories are works of fiction or true historical accounts, yet they can be thought-provoking and engaging.

Relationships and Connections Throughout Lives One of the main tenets of the concept of past lives is the notion that relationships and connections can endure throughout lifetimes. People frequently tell stories of running into people in this life who they had close relationships with in previous lives. This may show itself as acute feelings, immediate identification, or even unresolved issues from past lifetimes.

The idea that our relationships with others can be woven into the fabric of our soul's journey and extend beyond our current lifetime is emphasized by the belief in these karmic ties.

UNRESOLVED PROBLEMS AND KARMIC LESSONS

According to many reincarnation proponents, karmic lessons and unresolved difficulties are essential to the human experience. According to the idea, people reincarnate to continue their spiritual development. Resolving unfinished business from past lifetimes or dealing with the fallout from past deeds are common themes in past life recollections. One approach to progress and eventually reach higher spiritual enlightenment is through this procedure. This viewpoint heavily relies on the idea of karma, which holds that the repercussions of our deeds carry over into the next life.

Investigating former lives and the memories connected to them is a challenging and profoundly spiritual undertaking. These ideas continue to pique people's interest because they present a distinctive viewpoint on the nature of consciousness, personal development, and the interconnection of all living things over time and space even though they may not be widely acknowledged or supported by science.

CHAPTER FOUR

THE PAST LIFE REGRESSION THERAPY PROCESS

GETTING READY FOR A PAST LIFE REGRESSION CONSULTATION

Through the intriguing and frequently profoundly spiritual practice of past life regression therapy, people can learn more about their former incarnations and acquire an understanding of the difficulties and problems of the present. It is important to prepare well before engaging in a past life regression session. The therapist and the client are both involved in this preparation.

PREPARING THE SCENE

Setting up a welcoming and cozy space is essential to a successful past-life regression session. To help the client unwind, the therapy room should be quiet, distraction-free, and have calming décor and lighting. To guarantee that the customer can effortlessly enter a hypnotic state, comfortable seats or a therapeutic couch are utilized. To establish a calm environment and make their clients feel more at ease during the regression, many therapists use items like essential oils or calming music.

ASSESSMENT AND INTAKE OF CLIENTS

Past life regression therapy begins with a thorough client intake and screening procedure. The client's current problems, worries, and session objectives should be ascertained by the therapist. To customize the regression experience to the client's needs, this information is essential. Furthermore, knowing the client's mental and emotional state aids the therapist in deciding whether previous life regression is the right kind of treatment for the patient.

STRATEGIES AND PROCEDURES

Therapists who specialize in past-life regression use a variety of approaches and strategies to help their clients navigate the regression process. Hypnotherapy is a popular method that is used to create a trance-like, calm state. Clients can examine memories from previous lives and tap into their subconscious during this stage. Other techniques that assist clients in connecting with their former life experiences without the aid of outside counsel are self-hypnosis and guided visualization.

REGRESSION AND HYPNOSIS

A key component of former life regression therapy is hypnotherapy. The process of inducing a hypnotic state facilitates the client's access to their subconscious by making their conscious mind more calm and responsive. In addition to assisting the client with relaxation techniques, the therapist helps them access memories and experiences from previous lives. Deepening procedures to improve the link with the past life are frequently part of the process.

ASSISTED DISPLAY

One typical technique in former life regression therapy is guided visualization. The client is asked to visualize particular situations or scenes from their previous life by the therapist. These images can act as portals to memories and feelings from previous lives. The client can traverse these images and learn important facts about their past incarnations with the assistance of the therapist.

SELF-HYPNOSIS FOR INVESTIGATING PAST LIVES

Although therapists frequently lead their patients through regression and hypnosis, some people also use self-hypnosis methods to investigate their past lives on their own. These patients can use self-hypnosis to access memories from previous lives, but effective outcomes typically need a lot of practice and self-control.

THE THERAPIST'S FUNCTION

In former life regression, the therapist is an essential facilitator of the entire process. In addition to establishing a secure and welcoming space, the therapist needs to establish rapport and trust with the client. For the client to feel comfortable and open about sharing their memories and feelings throughout the regression, this trust is necessary.

ESTABLISHING RAPPORT AND TRUST

In previous life regression therapy, the therapist and the client must develop a relationship based on trust. To make sure the client feels safe and supported during the session, the therapist must build a professional and compassionate rapport. The client can examine their past lives, be more open, and share their feelings and experiences when they feel trusted.

ENCOURAGING REGRESSION

The therapist leads the client through visualization or hypnosis techniques during the regression process. To help the client describe their prior life experiences, find pertinent facts, and get insight into the lessons and themes that might be influencing their current life, they pose probing inquiries. The therapist's job is to assist and encourage the exploration while remaining impartial and nonjudgmental.

MANAGING THE RELEASE OF EMOTIONS

Clients undergoing previous life regression therapy frequently experience strong emotions associated with their former life experiences. The therapist needs to be ready to handle these outpouring of emotion with compassion and consideration. Whether the client is experiencing trauma, happiness, or sadness, the therapist's job is to help them process and heal by creating a safe space in which they can express their feelings.

Previous life regression treatment is a singular and life-changing experience that necessitates meticulous planning, expert supervision, and a thorough comprehension of the therapeutic procedure. It includes setting up a comfortable setting, completing in-depth client intake and assessment, using a variety of strategies, and assisting with emotional release. To help clients examine their former lives and acquire important insights into their present-day issues and personal progress, the therapist plays a crucial role in developing rapport, and trust, and steering the regression process.

CHAPTER FIVE

HANDLING MEMORIES OF FORMER LIVES

For individuals who are open to investigating the idea of previous lifetimes or who believe in reincarnation, Navigating Past Life Memories can be a powerful and life-changing experience. Even though the idea of former life memories is still debatable and lacks scientific validation, many people find value and understanding in investigating these experiences as a way to further their personal development and self-discovery.

INTERPRETING PRIOR LIFE EXPERIENCES

Examining the memories and feelings connected to prior life experiences is necessary to interpret them. These memories might manifest as intense feelings of attachment to a specific place or time, vivid dreams, or déjà vu experiences.

People frequently use regression therapy, meditation, or spiritual practices to explain these experiences. To gain insight into the chances and challenges they face in their current existence, they could search for recurrent aspects, themes, or patterns in their memories of prior lives. Gaining an understanding of the significance of these experiences can help one grow personally and gain insights into their spiritual journey.

EXAMINING SYMBOLISM AND METAPHORS

Recollections of past lives are frequently rich in symbolism and metaphors, which call for close examination. These metaphors and symbols could indicate deeper psychological or emotional themes rather than being accurate depictions of historical events. For example, coming across the water in a former life recollection would not always indicate drowning; instead, it could represent emotional instability or the need for purification in the present life.

People can learn more about the lessons from previous incarnations they carry with them and how they apply them to their current situation by analyzing these symbols and metaphors.

ENDING UNFINISHED BUSINESS

The notion of ending unfinished business is one of the main drivers for investigating memories from a previous life. Unresolved matters, unfinished business in relationships, or unpaid karmic obligations from previous lifetimes might follow a person into this one. People seek closure, healing, and a sense of fulfillment by admitting and dealing with these unsolved issues. By letting go of the weight of the past, this approach can promote personal growth and a sense of release.

HEALING AND TRAUMA

Delving into memories from a previous life can be a double-edged sword since it can force people to face trauma from a previous existence. Past-life traumas might show up as bodily or mental suffering in the here and now. Regression therapy, energy healing, or meditation are gentle and therapeutic methods for addressing past life trauma. Recognizing and letting go of these old traumas is the goal to facilitate emotional recovery and personal development during this lifetime.

HANDLING PAST LIFE TRAUMA

Handling past life memories requires addressing past life trauma. An individual's conduct, relationships, and general well-being can be impacted by traumatic memories in the present. Regression therapists, hypnotists, and psychologists assist people in processing and letting go of traumas from previous lives. One may get increased emotional resilience and inner serenity in their current life as a result of this life-changing and cathartic experience.

CHAPTER SIX

COMBINATION AND MODIFICATION
INCLUDING LIFE AFTER LIFE TEACHINGS
IN DAILY ACTIVITIES

The process of transferring the knowledge and experiences from previous lifetimes into this one is known as "past life integration." The notions of reincarnation and the idea that our souls have lived several lives before to this one are widely accepted. Gaining knowledge or recollections from these previous incarnations might offer significant perspectives on one's present life experience. People frequently meditate, undergo regression treatment, or just think back on their intuitions and reoccurring patterns to integrate these insights. They hope to gain a deeper understanding of who they are, what they have chosen, and why they are here. A more fulfilled existence, as well as personal development and self-awareness, might result from this integration.

WISDOM AND LESSONS

Wisdom and lessons from previous lives are seen as important resources for direction and personal growth. It is believed that during many lifetimes, our souls gather wisdom and knowledge, which we bring with us into each subsequent incarnation. Making better decisions in this life can be aided by thinking back on lessons learned in previous ones. It can also shed light on relationships, skills, or reoccurring problems that we have carried over. People who comprehend these lessons can intentionally use them to handle their current circumstances with more resilience and knowledge.

CREATING NEW GOALS

A crucial first step toward personal development is making new intentions based on lessons learned from former lives. It entails making the conscious decision to match one's present desires and life goals with the knowledge acquired from previous lifetimes. For example, someone may decide to pursue a creative career or hobby in this life if they find a recurrent theme of self-expression or creativity in previous lives. People can live more truly and in alignment with their soul's purpose by doing this, which can lead to a profound sense of fulfillment.

THE EFFECT ON SYSTEMS OF BELIEF

An individual's belief systems may be significantly impacted by the incorporation of knowledge from previous lives. Given that it implies that the soul's journey is more than a single lifetime, it frequently contradicts conventional religious or cultural views. Those who accept these realizations might develop a more diverse and open-minded spiritual viewpoint. However incorporating insights from previous lives might also encounter opposition and skepticism, especially in societies that reject the idea of reincarnation. People must travel this path with awareness and consideration for both their own and other people's belief systems.

CHANGING CONCEPTS

A paradigm shift occurs when past life experiences lead to a fundamental reconceptualization of one's life, purpose, and existence. It may result in a viewpoint on life that is more integrated and holistic. People may start to perceive their previous incarnations as interrelated stages in their spiritual development, each playing a part in their personal growth. A deeper comprehension of the connectivity of all living things and a stronger sense of oneness with the universe may result from this paradigm shift.

BRINGING BELIEFS FROM A PAST LIFE INTO THE PRESENT

It can be a difficult and sometimes confusing process to reconcile beliefs from previous lives with the realities of the present. It entails striking a balance between the practical requirements of one's current existence and the lessons learned from previous lives. Some people could have trouble making sense of their current situation about their former lives, particularly if there are significant discrepancies or contradictions. It's critical to tackle this with an open mind and heart, looking for methods to balance applying the knowledge from the past with managing the reality of the present. A deeper feeling of purpose in life and personal growth can result from this process, which has the potential to be extremely transforming.

CHAPTER SEVEN

DISPUTATIONS AND REACTIONS
DOUBT AND SCIENTIFIC DISCUSSION

The scientific method is inherently based on skepticism, which propels the progress of scientific understanding. Scientists are taught to examine presumptions and require proof to support any theory, approaching new concepts and assertions with a critical perspective. Sustaining the integrity of the scientific method depends on this skepticism. It makes sure that unsupported statements are rejected and that only hypotheses that have undergone extensive testing and support are allowed. In addition, skepticism encourages constructive scientific disagreement, which is crucial for enhancing and perfecting our comprehension of the natural world.

The process of challenging established hypotheses and putting out new ones through intense, sometimes contentious conversations is known as scientific debate. This ongoing conversation promotes the creation of more precise explanations and highlights the shortcomings in the models that are currently in use. An excellent illustration of a scientific argument is the current discussion about climate change. Discussions about manmade global warming are held between climate scientists environmentalists and skeptics who challenge the consensus. Although skepticism can occasionally stem from ideological or political motivations, it is crucial to examine scientific assertions and make sure they hold up to close examination.

SCIENTIFIC JUSTIFICATIONS AND REBUTTALS

The methodical process of formulating scientific explanations involves data collecting, experimentation, observation, and the application of preexisting rules and ideas. The fact that these explanations are open to examination and criticism is essential to the advancement of science. There are many different ways to criticize research: you might challenge the validity of data or the interpretation of findings, or you can criticize experimental procedures. It is critical to recognize that scientific theories are subject to change in the face of strong evidence or well-reasoned arguments.

Scientific explanations that are criticized frequently result in better knowledge and improved models. The evolution of the atomic theory over time serves as an example of this process. Older theories, like Dalton's atomic theory, were challenged and updated when new data and understandings became available. A great deal of scientific discussion and criticism led to the development of the Bohr model and, subsequently, the quantum mechanical model of the atom.

These developments in atomic theory show how scientific progress is propelled forward by criticism.

CONSIDERING ETHICS

Science's ethical concerns involve a wide range of topics, from subject care and research procedures to the possible ramifications of scientific findings. Scientists need to make choices that put people's welfare, society's welfare, and the environment first. They also need to be acutely aware of the ethical consequences of their work. The use of human subjects in scientific research is a topic of intense ethical controversy. The Nuremberg Code, which was created during the World War II Nuremberg Trials, stressed participant welfare and informed consent while laying the groundwork for ethical standards in human research.

Concerns regarding cloning, gene editing, and the possibility of unexpected effects are at the forefront of ethical debates surrounding genetic engineering and biotechnology. The emergence of technologies such as CRISPR-Cas9 has prompted discussions over the morality of altering human DNA and the possibility of producing genetically modified offspring. The possible advantages and disadvantages of these technologies, as well as the societal ramifications of their broad use, must be carefully considered in the ethical debate around them.

The scientific method relies heavily on skepticism and scientific debate to ensure that hypotheses and explanations are put to the test and improved. Criticism of scientific explanations is a process that improves models and deepens our understanding of the natural world.

CHAPTER EIGHT

BEYOND REGRESSION TO PAST LIVES

Regression therapy has multiple therapeutic uses outside of previous life regression that delves into various facets of an individual's awareness and experiences. These apps present special chances for recovery, introspection, and personal development. Future advancement and life between lifetimes regression are two particularly interesting and perceptive methods among them.

ADDITIONAL THERAPEUTIC USES

Regression therapy is being used for a variety of therapeutic goals by practitioners, going beyond the investigation of former incarnations. Regression therapy is used by some people to treat current problems like anxiety, phobias, and unsolved emotional traumas. Clients can learn more about the underlying causes of their current difficulties by going back and revisiting formative experiences or important life events.

FUTURE ADVANCEMENT

Regression therapy is carried into the future with future progression, as the name implies, as a therapeutic application. It investigates the idea that people can access and learn about their future selves and experiences. Future advancement proponents contend that human consciousness transcends linear time, notwithstanding possible criticism. They contend that it is feasible to discover prospective life routes and to access future possibilities.

Clients are guided to de-stress and experience a profound level of awareness throughout subsequent progression sessions. They might meet their future selves, see glimpses of their lives in the future, or learn about important future events from this state. Offering clients a more comprehensive view of their life's path is the aim rather than making predictions about particular results. This can assist people in planning for future possibilities and problems as well as helping them make better decisions in the here and now.

REGRESSION OF LIFE BETWEEN LIVES

Regression to life between lives is a powerful therapeutic technique that investigates the spiritual plane that occurs between life on Earth. Dr. Michael Newton, who documented thousands of cases in his studies on life between lifetimes experiences, popularized this technique. To access the memories and insights of their existence in the spiritual realm between lives, entails guiding them into a deep, hypnotic condition.

Clients who undergo life between lifetimes regression frequently report seeing their soul group or soulmates, connecting with spiritual guides, and reflecting on the meaning of their previous lives and current ones. People who go through this process may have a greater awareness of their soul's journey, the lessons they are meant to acquire, and their relationships with other souls.

Regression to a life between lifetimes can be a profoundly healing and transformational experience. It can assist people in discovering their life's purpose, establishing a connection with their higher self, and experiencing inner calm and spiritual development. It is frequently viewed as a means of delving into higher states of consciousness and gaining knowledge that might inform one's choices and actions in the here and now.

Regression therapy offers a range of therapeutic applications that go beyond past life regression and can offer significant insights into an individual's past, present, and future experiences. Future advancement and life between-lives regression explore the potential and spiritual domains, providing special chances for self-discovery, healing, and personal development.

In the end, these methods enable a deeper comprehension of one's life's purpose and journey by encouraging people to delve into the depths of their awareness and the connectivity of their experiences throughout time and dimensions.